THE ADVENTUROUS KID'S GUIDE TO

THE
WORLD'S MOST
MYSTERIOUS
PLACES

WRITTEN BY
PATRICK MAKIN

ILLUSTRATED BY
WHOOLI CHEN

WARNING

Restricted Area

PHOTOGRAPHY
OF THIS AREA
IS PROHIBITED

RESTRICTED AREA

NO TRESPASSING
BEYOND THIS
POINT

MILITARY
INSTALLATION
OFF LIMITS TO
UNAUTHORIZED PERSONNEL

MAGIC CAT 🐱 PUBLISHING

NEW YORK

WHERE DO YOU WANT TO GO?

The world is more mysterious than you think.

In this age of information and exploration, the world may seem more accessible than ever . . . but some places remain off-limits, no matter how hard you try to get there. Some are physically impossible to reach. Others are too dangerous to visit, while others still contain mysteries so secret that they're hidden from the world. And the location of some of the most tantalizing places of all are lost and have been consigned to history . . . until now.

With your magic carpet, you are able to fly to Earth's remotest corners, discover sights unseen for hundreds of years, and explore the truth behind its most enigmatic sites.

Just be sure to bring your sense of wonder with you.

CONTENTS

BOUVET ISLAND

- South Atlantic Ocean -

THE REMOTEST PLACE ON EARTH

There are many reasons why Bouvet Island doesn't receive many visitors. For one thing, the island is just under 19 square miles of uninhabited ice sitting on a volcano in the middle of the freezing South Atlantic Ocean. Then there's the fact that it is surrounded by steep cliffs and some of the roughest seas on the planet. A scientific research station located here was also destroyed in an earthquake in 2006. But the main reason not very many people visit is because Bouvet Island is the remotest island on the planet . . . Not an easy trip—even if you have a magic carpet to get there!

DIVERSE WILDLIFE

Although uninhabited by humans, Bouvet Island is home to plenty of wildlife, including albatrosses, snow petrels, fur seals, and hundreds of chinstrap and macaroni penguins. Since 1971, the island and its surrounding waters have been classified as a nature reserve.

THE FIRST VOYAGE

The island was first spotted by the French explorer Jean-Baptiste Charles Bouvet de Lozier during an Antarctic expedition in 1739. The voyage was so demanding that most of the crew fell ill, and, with dwindling supplies, Jean-Baptiste had to call off the expedition before he could set foot on land. Worse still, the wrong coordinates were noted down—meaning no one could find it again for another 69 years!

AQUATIC LIFE

Lucky visitors to the island can see orcas (also known as killer whales) and humpback whales swimming close to its shores.

HUMAN CONTACT

No one lives on Bouvet Island because the conditions are too harsh to support human life. One of the few explorations of the island, in 1964, came across a whaler's lifeboat washed up on the shore of its jagged coastline. The boat still contained supplies, but no other signs of life were found.

TOTAL ISOLATION

Bouvet Island lies over 1,000 miles away from the nearest landmass—Antarctica—and approximately 1,400 miles from the nearest inhabited land mass, Tristan da Cunha . . . which is itself another of the remotest islands in the world.

FLYING THE FLAG

Since 1930, Bouvet Island has been owned by Norway, which is more than 8,000 miles away.

In Norwegian, the island is called Bouvetøya, in honor of Jean-Baptiste.

ARENAL VOLCANO

- Alajuela Province, Costa Rica -

THE FORBIDDEN RAINFOREST

Costa Rica's Arenal Volcano might currently be dormant but visitors still aren't allowed anywhere close to its crater. Despite looking like a paradise for wildlife, a quick glance down to the rainforest below will reveal vents releasing 392°F gases and jagged paths left by tumbling rocks as big as houses! Be prepared to make a quick getaway: Just because Arenal is dormant now, that doesn't mean things can't suddenly change. In 1968, after 400 years of inactivity, the volcano erupted without warning and completely destroyed three villages, leaving a trail of havoc in its wake.

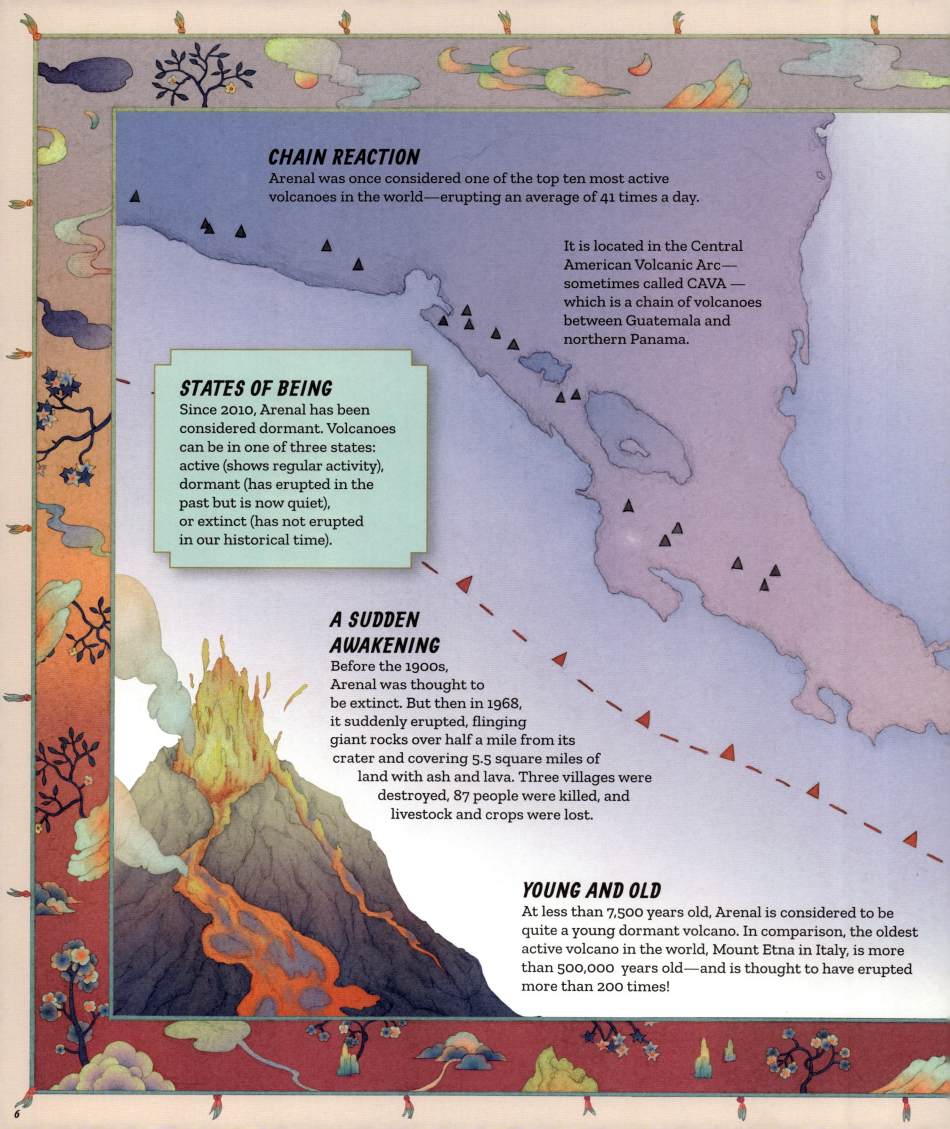

CHAIN REACTION

Arenal was once considered one of the top ten most active volcanoes in the world—erupting an average of 41 times a day.

It is located in the Central American Volcanic Arc—sometimes called CAVA —which is a chain of volcanoes between Guatemala and northern Panama.

STATES OF BEING

Since 2010, Arenal has been considered dormant. Volcanoes can be in one of three states: active (shows regular activity), dormant (has erupted in the past but is now quiet), or extinct (has not erupted in our historical time).

A SUDDEN AWAKENING

Before the 1900s, Arenal was thought to be extinct. But then in 1968, it suddenly erupted, flinging giant rocks over half a mile from its crater and covering 5.5 square miles of land with ash and lava. Three villages were destroyed, 87 people were killed, and livestock and crops were lost.

YOUNG AND OLD

At less than 7,500 years old, Arenal is considered to be quite a young dormant volcano. In comparison, the oldest active volcano in the world, Mount Etna in Italy, is more than 500,000 years old—and is thought to have erupted more than 200 times!

DEADLY VENOM

The highly venomous Bothrops asper is just one of several species of snake found in the foothills of the volcano. Able to grow up to 8.2 feet in length, a bite from this deadly snake can lead to gangrene—or worse. So keep your feet tucked up on your magic carpet as you explore!

BIRD'S EYE VIEW

Despite its fiery reputation, the national park containing the Arenal Volcano is home to plenty of wildlife. More than 500 species of birds are found here, including toucans and hummingbirds.

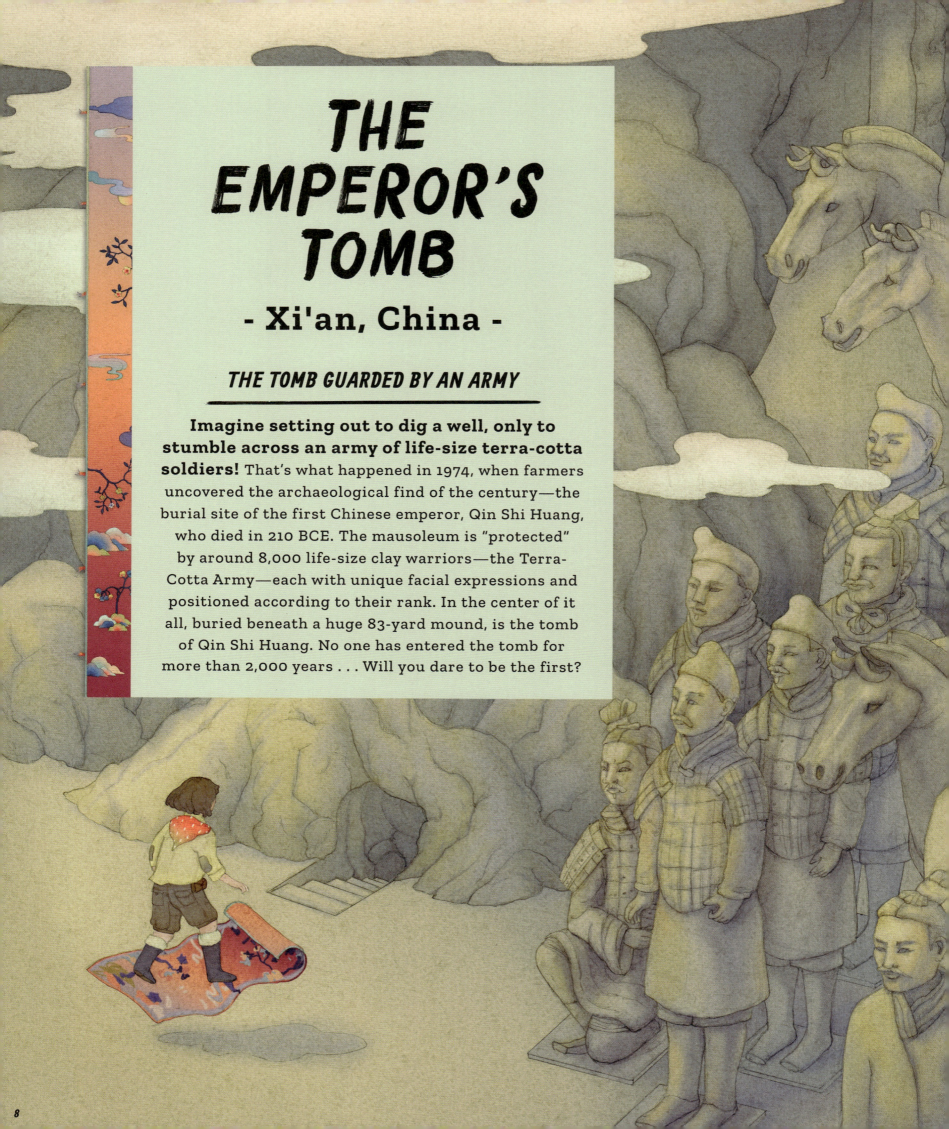

THE EMPEROR'S TOMB

- Xi'an, China -

THE TOMB GUARDED BY AN ARMY

Imagine setting out to dig a well, only to stumble across an army of life-size terra-cotta soldiers! That's what happened in 1974, when farmers uncovered the archaeological find of the century—the burial site of the first Chinese emperor, Qin Shi Huang, who died in 210 BCE. The mausoleum is "protected" by around 8,000 life-size clay warriors—the Terra-Cotta Army—each with unique facial expressions and positioned according to their rank. In the center of it all, buried beneath a huge 83-yard mound, is the tomb of Qin Shi Huang. No one has entered the tomb for more than 2,000 years . . . Will you dare to be the first?

THE FIRST DYNASTY

In 221 BCE, ruler of Qin state Qin Shi Huang conquered six states at war to create the first unified nation of China and became its first emperor. He died 11 years later, in 210 BCE.

AN ENTIRE ARMY

According to archaeologists, the Terra-Cotta Army was built to accompany Qin Shi Huang into the afterlife and protect him thereafter. The garrison consisted of an estimated 8,000 soldiers, 130 chariots, and 650 horses.

THE ELIXIR OF LIFE

It is thought that the tomb itself could contain a three dimensional map of China with lakes and rivers of liquid mercury, which the ancient Chinese believed could help one live forever. Qin Shi Huang did everything he could to find the elixir of life and achieve immortality, but not even the first emperor of China could outrun death.

PIECE BY PIECE

It is said that more than 700,000 laborers worked on the army. Individual parts of the body were constructed in workshops before being sealed together with a substance called lute. Craftsmen were responsible for creating individual facial features. Finally, each figure was placed in a precise location, depending on its rank and role.

ETERNAL ENTERTAINERS

Not all the figures are soldiers. Pits dug around the tomb have revealed clay dancers, musicians, and acrobats—all full of life and mid-performance. Each figure is said to have its own unique facial expression and was once brightly painted, before the colors faded over time.

EXCAVATION AND PRESERVATION

Archaeologists don't want to open the tomb of Qin Shi Huang until the technology is advanced enough to preserve everything they might find inside. It is possible that the tomb will never be excavated because the Chinese government may choose to respect the burial rites of their first emperor.

POVEGLIA

- Venice, Italy -

THE HAUNTED ISLAND

Venice is known as one of the most romantic places on Earth. But as you soar through the sky above Venice's lagoon, you'll discover a different story on Poveglia. In the late 1700s, this small uninhabited island was used as a place to confine— and then bury—people dying from the plague. The buildings were then converted into a psychiatric hospital, and Poveglia has been closed to visitors since the hospital shut down, in 1968. Today, the "Island of No Return" has a reputation as one of the most haunted places in Italy.

ONE-WAY TICKET

The island first became a quarantine station for people with the plague in 1793. It was used as a hospital for anyone believed to be ill with the disease, so the healthy could be separated from the sick.

If you were taken to Poveglia, the chances of you leaving were very slim. Over 100,000 people were buried on the island.

THE DOCTOR

The psychiatric hospital was apparently run by a doctor who performed nightmarish experiments on his patients. However, his reign was cut short when he fell from the twelfth-century bell tower and died. Legend says he was pushed by an evil spirit, and some say that the bell could still be heard tolling years after it had been removed from the tower altogether!

A SANCTUARY

Originally, Poveglia hosted Italians seeking to escape invasions in nearby cities and towns in 421 BCE. However, in 1379, Poveglia itself came under attack from an enemy navy and its inhabitants were moved to Giudecca—another island in the Venetian Lagoon—leaving Poveglia deserted.

NATURE RETURNS

The abandoned hospital still stands, despite the fact that it closed more than 50 years ago. The buildings are now covered in plants that grow up the crumbling walls and through the broken windows, slowly consuming the supposedly haunted structures.

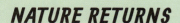

A FANCY FUTURE

In recent years, the Italian government had been trying to sell the island, hoping that someone might turn the hospital into a luxury hotel, but no sale has been announced yet, despite the fact that Venice is one of the most popular tourist destinations in the world. Strange . . .

VENDESI

CLOSE ENOUGH

Since it's closed to visitors, Poveglia is the only place in the whole of the Venetian Lagoon that is not served by any public transportation. However, if you're brave enough you can book a boat tour, which is the closest you can get to this eerie mass burial site.

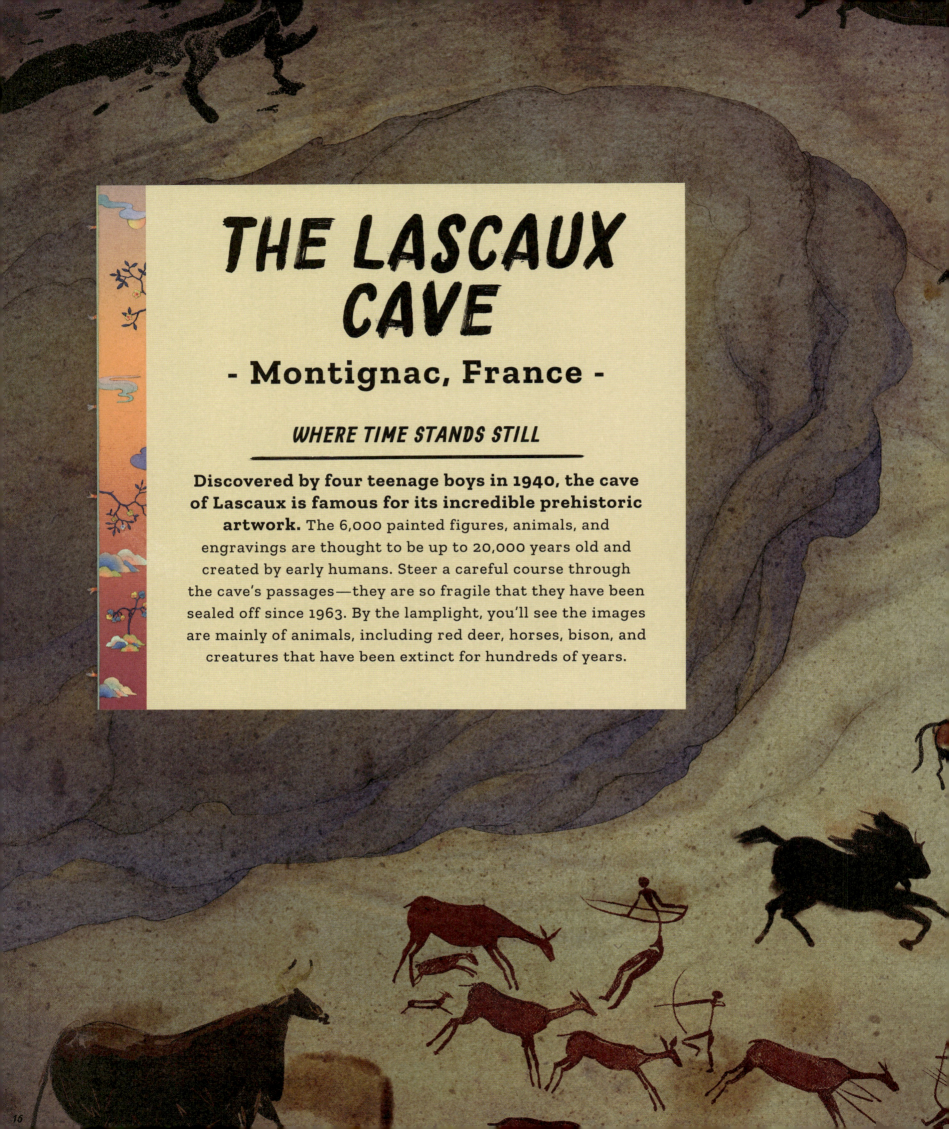

THE LASCAUX CAVE

- Montignac, France -

WHERE TIME STANDS STILL

Discovered by four teenage boys in 1940, the cave of Lascaux is famous for its incredible prehistoric artwork. The 6,000 painted figures, animals, and engravings are thought to be up to 20,000 years old and created by early humans. Steer a careful course through the cave's passages—they are so fragile that they have been sealed off since 1963. By the lamplight, you'll see the images are mainly of animals, including red deer, horses, bison, and creatures that have been extinct for hundreds of years.

MAN AND BEAST

The only image of a human in the cave shows a fight between a man and a bison in which the man appears to have been struck and the bison has been stabbed by a spear. Other paintings depict horses, ibex, lions, a bear, and an auroch (an extinct species of cattle last seen in 1627).

NOT-SO-FUN FUNGI

Opening the cave to the public caused the art inside to begin to fade and also led to the growth of fungi, bacteria, and crystals on the walls. This caused serious damage to the paintings. The cave was closed in 1963, but despite efforts to preserve the art, the fungi spread further into the cave. In 2009, 300 experts from around the world came together to find a solution and work on new ways to preserve the site continues to this day.

UNEXPECTED DISCOVERY

The cave was discovered on September 12, 1940, by 18-year-old Marcel Ravidat. He and his three friends discovered the cave just a few days after his dog, Robot, had fallen down a fox hole as they walked the hill of Lascaux. In 1979, the cave was added to the list of UNESCO World Heritage Sites.

THE NEXT BEST THING

Those without a magic carpet can visit Lascaux II, a perfect replica of the original cave. Opened in 1983, this replica cave is situated only 219 yards from the original.

ANCIENT VALLEY

The cave is close to an ancient town called Montignac, which is perched on the banks of the Vézère river. Another twenty-four decorated caves can be found in the Vézère valley . . . but none quite as impressive as Lascaux.

ANCIENT TECHNOLOGY

The artists that worked 20,000 years ago used different minerals to achieve the shades of color seen in the paintings: hematite was used for red and charcoal for black. They would have used their fingers, pieces of charcoal, or brushes made from hair to apply the pigments. Scientists think that they worked by the light of lamps, using animal fat as a fuel.

AREA 51

- Nevada, United States -

THE MYSTERIOUS MILITARY BASE

According to the U.S. government, Area 51 is a military base in Nevada where the U.S. Air Force tests top-secret combat aircraft. But is that true? As you silently soar through the desert night sky, see if you can spot anything. In 1989, Bob Lazar claimed that the U.S. government was keeping an alien spacecraft here, and that he saw a briefing document containing a photo of an alien. Since then, stories of alien visits, teleportation, and other strange activities have surfaced, which, of course, the U.S. government denies . . . But how can we be sure when Area 51 is off limits to the public and under twenty-four-hour guard?

WARNING
Restricted Area
PHOTOGRAPHY OF THIS AREA IS PROHIBITED

ING!
SPASSING
ALLATION

RESTRICTED AREA
NO TRESPASSING
BEYOND THIS POINT

MILITARY INSTALLATION
OFF LIMITS TO UNAUTHORIZED PERSONNEL

THE FIRST UFOs

Conspiracies first began to surface about alien aircraft in 1947 when a UFO (unidentified flying object) crashed into a ranch in the Roswell region of New Mexico. However, the U.S. military was quick to claim that the object was just a weather balloon.

MILITARY SECRETS

In 1955, according to the U.S. government, the area was chosen as a testing site for the Lockheed U-2, a new aircraft designed for high-altitude military observation (spying). But officials only admitted that Area 51 even existed almost 60 years later, in 2013. Why all the secrecy?

OUTRAGEOUS CLAIMS

What really put Area 51 in the spotlight was a series of claims made by a man called Robert "Bob" Lazar. He stated that he had worked at S-4, a mysterious site near Area 51, where his job was to reverse-engineer flying saucers from space. Lazar was later said to be a fraud who lied about his employment at Area 51 and his entire education. But Lazar claimed the U.S. government had erased all of his records in an attempt to discredit his claims . . .

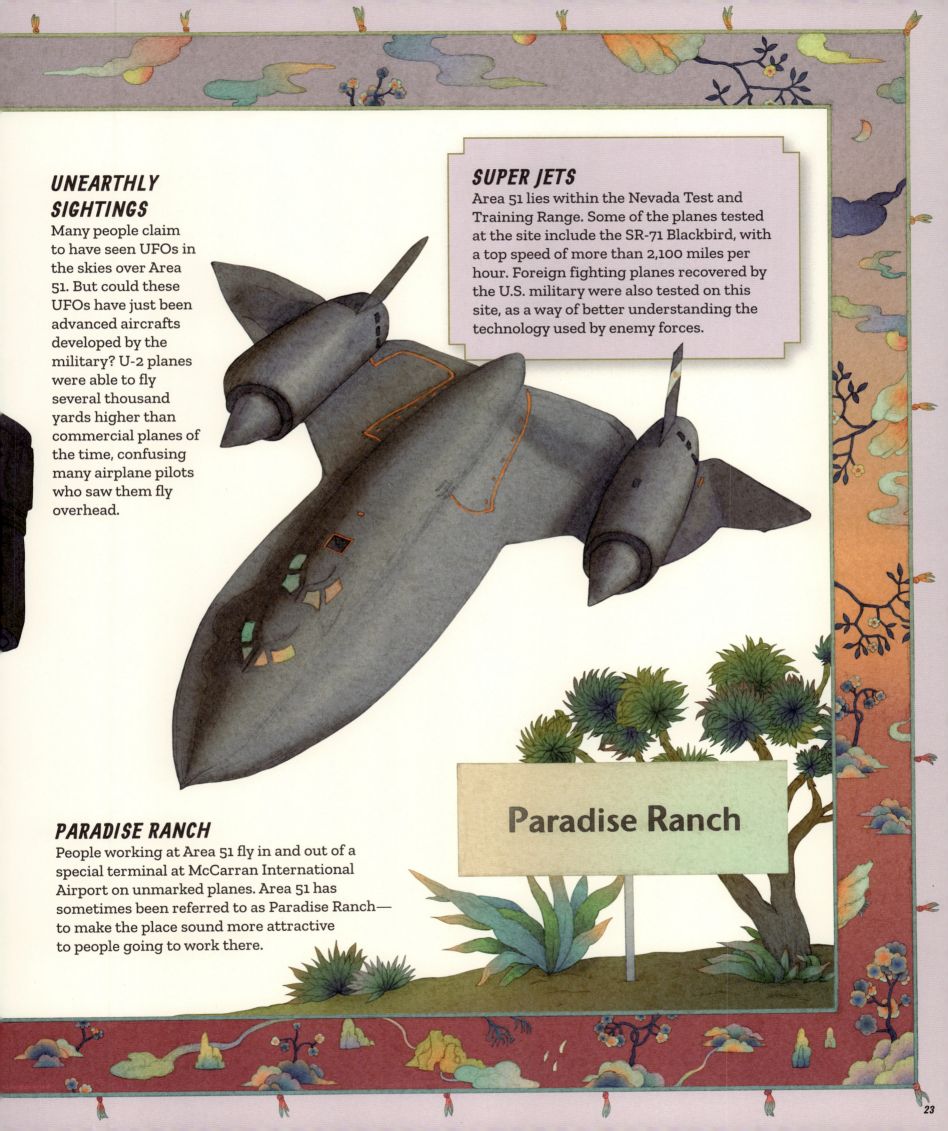

UNEARTHLY SIGHTINGS

Many people claim to have seen UFOs in the skies over Area 51. But could these UFOs have just been advanced aircrafts developed by the military? U-2 planes were able to fly several thousand yards higher than commercial planes of the time, confusing many airplane pilots who saw them fly overhead.

SUPER JETS

Area 51 lies within the Nevada Test and Training Range. Some of the planes tested at the site include the SR-71 Blackbird, with a top speed of more than 2,100 miles per hour. Foreign fighting planes recovered by the U.S. military were also tested on this site, as a way of better understanding the technology used by enemy forces.

PARADISE RANCH

People working at Area 51 fly in and out of a special terminal at McCarran International Airport on unmarked planes. Area 51 has sometimes been referred to as Paradise Ranch— to make the place sound more attractive to people going to work there.

Paradise Ranch

FULLY EQUIPPED

Air Force One has extra living quarters for those who accompany the president, as well as two food preparation galleys that can feed 100 people at a time. This is on top of a dining room and the president's bedroom and bathroom.

ONBOARD TECHNOLOGY

The commander-in-chief has everything they need on board to run the country, including secure communications equipment able to encrypt and scramble messages. There's also Wi-Fi, multifrequency radios, and 85 telephones! The plane also has its own conference room.

THE FLYING DOCTOR

A medical doctor attends every flight made by Air Force One. Inside the plane is a medical suite with its own operating table, two beds, and a full pharmacy, as well as resuscitation equipment in case anyone on board falls ill. If the president travels abroad, a full medical team (who have flown over in advance) awaits the president's arrival there, ready to take over in any emergency.

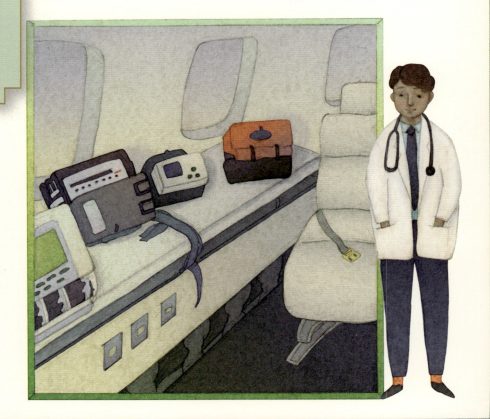

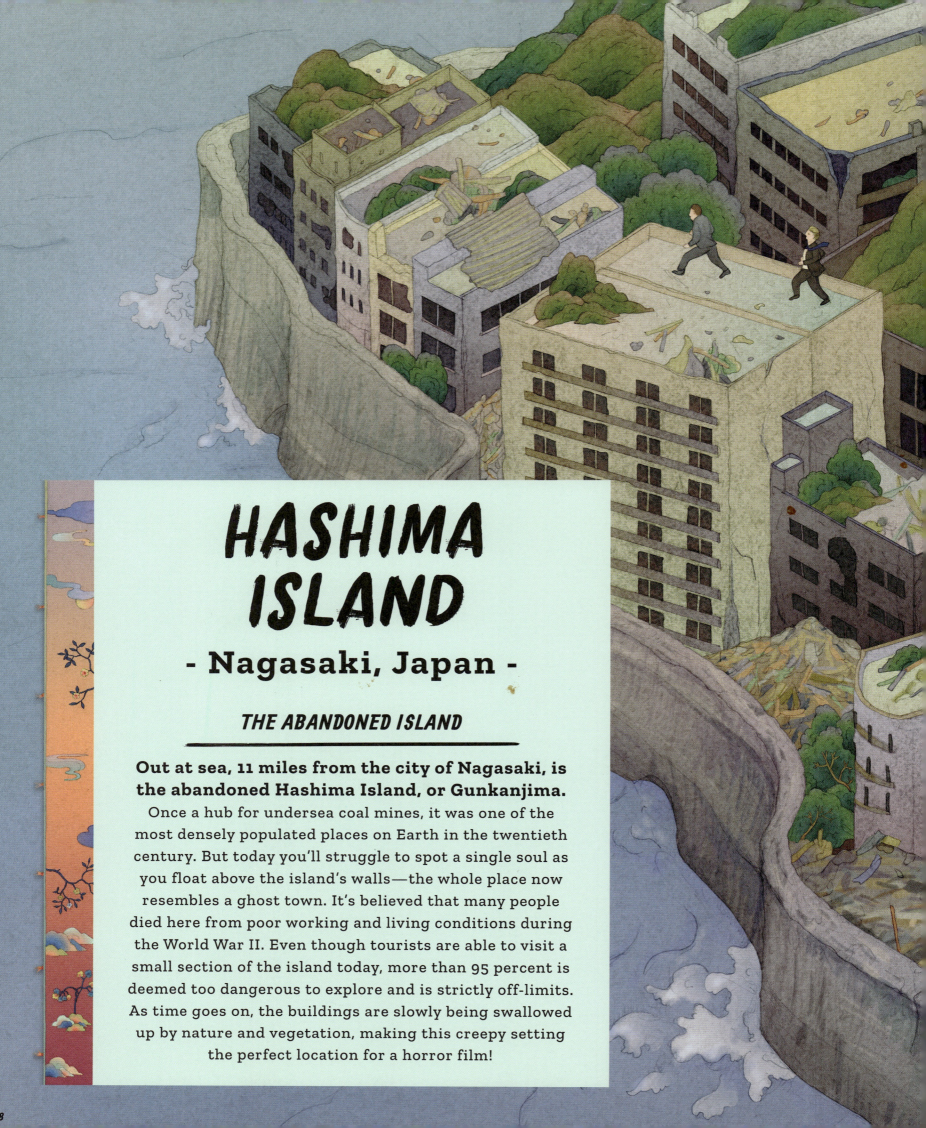

HASHIMA ISLAND

- Nagasaki, Japan -

THE ABANDONED ISLAND

Out at sea, 11 miles from the city of Nagasaki, is the abandoned Hashima Island, or Gunkanjima.
Once a hub for undersea coal mines, it was one of the most densely populated places on Earth in the twentieth century. But today you'll struggle to spot a single soul as you float above the island's walls—the whole place now resembles a ghost town. It's believed that many people died here from poor working and living conditions during the World War II. Even though tourists are able to visit a small section of the island today, more than 95 percent is deemed too dangerous to explore and is strictly off-limits. As time goes on, the buildings are slowly being swallowed up by nature and vegetation, making this creepy setting the perfect location for a horror film!

BLACK GOLD

Hashima Island was once the site of a thriving coal-mining operation—for almost a century, from 1887, it was filled with workers. In 1959, the population reached its peak of 5,259 people. But when the petroleum industry replaced the use of coal in the 1960s, the population gradually declined until the island's official closure in 1974.

A WORLD WONDER

Hashima Island is now a protected area and was made an official UNESCO World Heritage site in 2015. This recognizes the contribution it made to Japan's Industrial Revolution from the 1850s onwards.

BUILT TO LAST

In 1916, a seven-floor apartment block was built for workers. It was the first large, reinforced concrete building in Japan and was built in a way that could withstand damage from a typhoon.

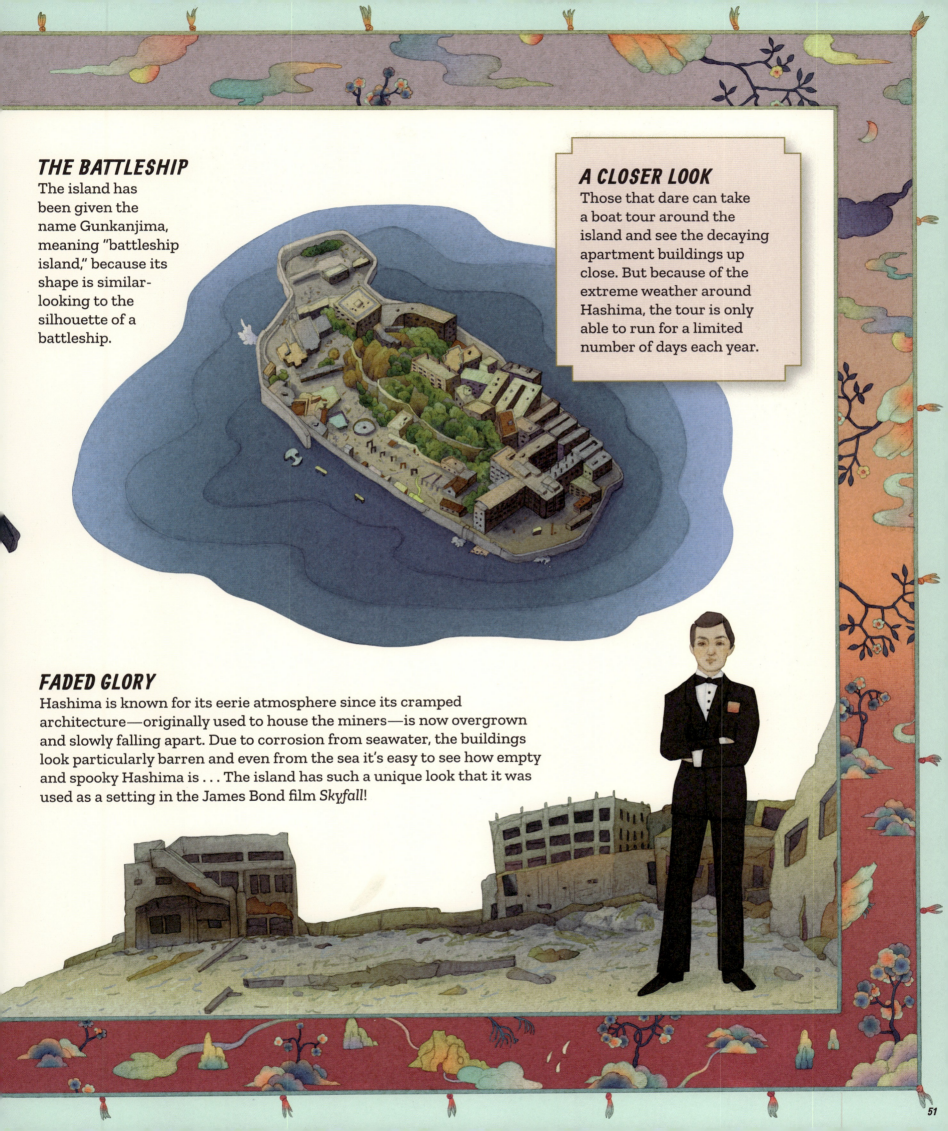

THE BATTLESHIP

The island has been given the name Gunkanjima, meaning "battleship island," because its shape is similar-looking to the silhouette of a battleship.

A CLOSER LOOK

Those that dare can take a boat tour around the island and see the decaying apartment buildings up close. But because of the extreme weather around Hashima, the tour is only able to run for a limited number of days each year.

FADED GLORY

Hashima is known for its eerie atmosphere since its cramped architecture—originally used to house the miners—is now overgrown and slowly falling apart. Due to corrosion from seawater, the buildings look particularly barren and even from the sea it's easy to see how empty and spooky Hashima is . . . The island has such a unique look that it was used as a setting in the James Bond film *Skyfall*!

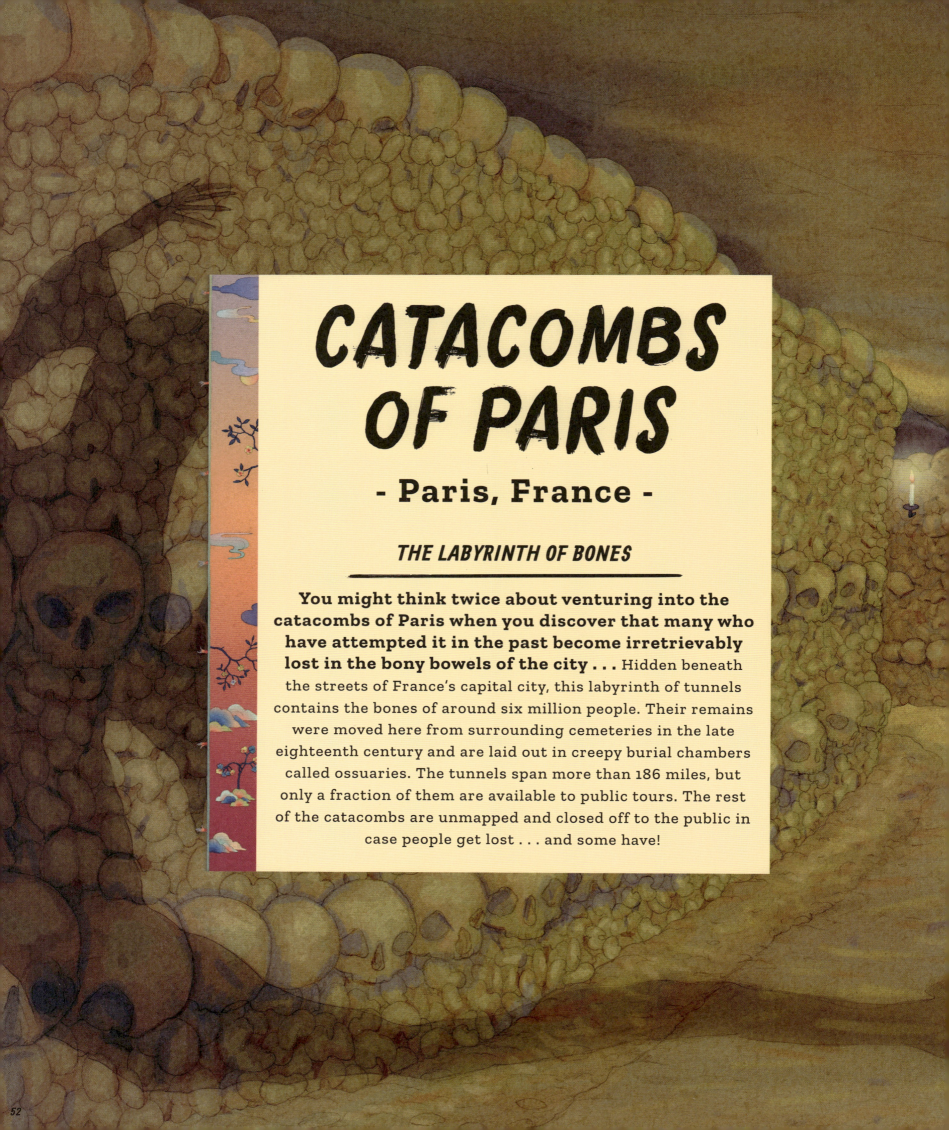

CATACOMBS OF PARIS

- Paris, France -

THE LABYRINTH OF BONES

You might think twice about venturing into the catacombs of Paris when you discover that many who have attempted it in the past become irretrievably lost in the bony bowels of the city . . . Hidden beneath the streets of France's capital city, this labyrinth of tunnels contains the bones of around six million people. Their remains were moved here from surrounding cemeteries in the late eighteenth century and are laid out in creepy burial chambers called ossuaries. The tunnels span more than 186 miles, but only a fraction of them are available to public tours. The rest of the catacombs are unmapped and closed off to the public in case people get lost . . . and some have!

OSSEMENTS·DU
CIMETIÈRE·DES
INNOCENTS·
DEPOSES·EN
AVRIL·1788

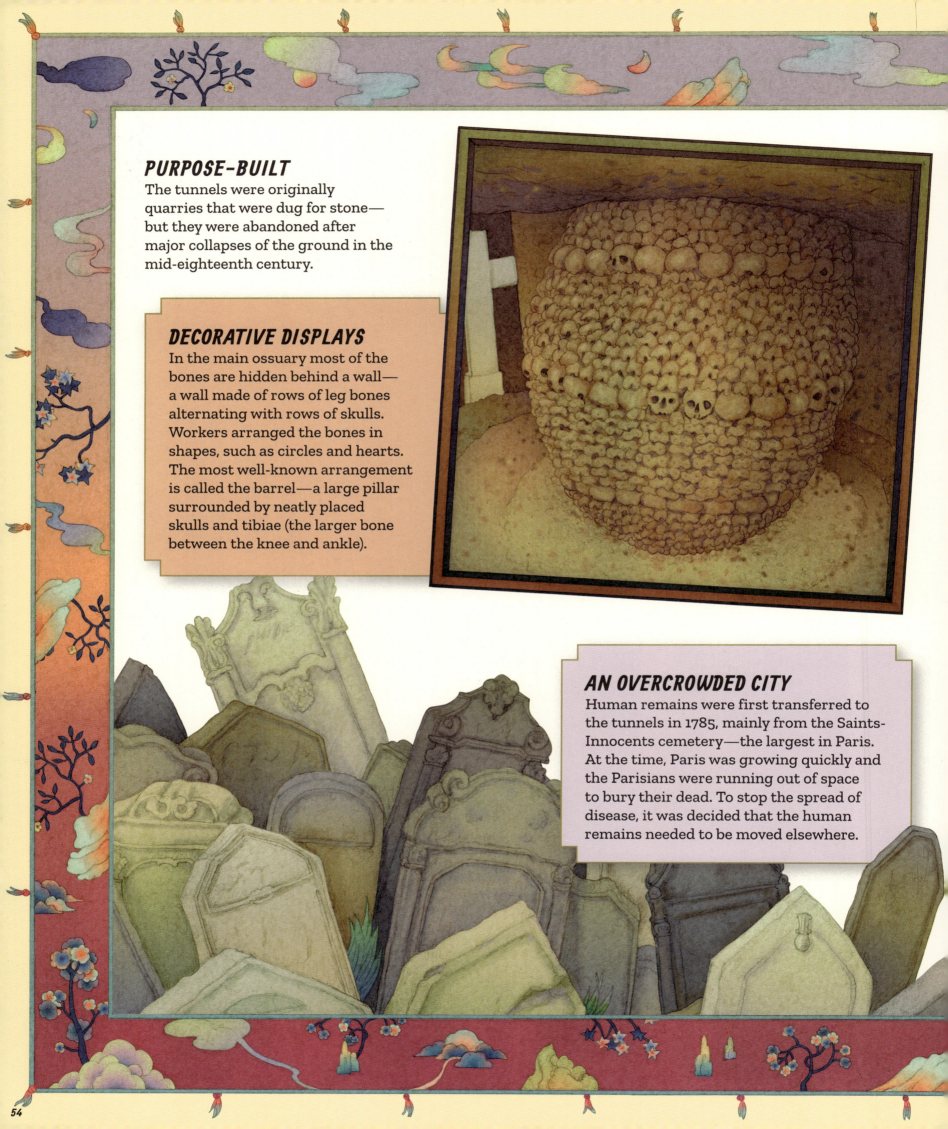

PURPOSE-BUILT

The tunnels were originally quarries that were dug for stone—but they were abandoned after major collapses of the ground in the mid-eighteenth century.

DECORATIVE DISPLAYS

In the main ossuary most of the bones are hidden behind a wall—a wall made of rows of leg bones alternating with rows of skulls. Workers arranged the bones in shapes, such as circles and hearts. The most well-known arrangement is called the barrel—a large pillar surrounded by neatly placed skulls and tibiae (the larger bone between the knee and ankle).

AN OVERCROWDED CITY

Human remains were first transferred to the tunnels in 1785, mainly from the Saints-Innocents cemetery—the largest in Paris. At the time, Paris was growing quickly and the Parisians were running out of space to bury their dead. To stop the spread of disease, it was decided that the human remains needed to be moved elsewhere.

A ROMAN NAMESAKE

The catacombs were named after the sixty-or-so ancient underground burial places found under the city of Rome.

GETTING LOST

The catacombs were opened to the public in 1809 and became a huge draw . . . for the living and the dead. In 2017, two teenagers were rescued and treated for hypothermia after being lost in the catacombs for three days.

SECRET SOCIETIES

All kinds of secretive activities have taken place in the catacombs over the centuries. In 2004, police ventured beyond a sign that said, "Building site: no access" and triggered a recording of guard dogs barking. They then discovered a huge 4,300-square-foot cave housing a full-size cinema, with amphitheater-style seating carved into the rock floor.

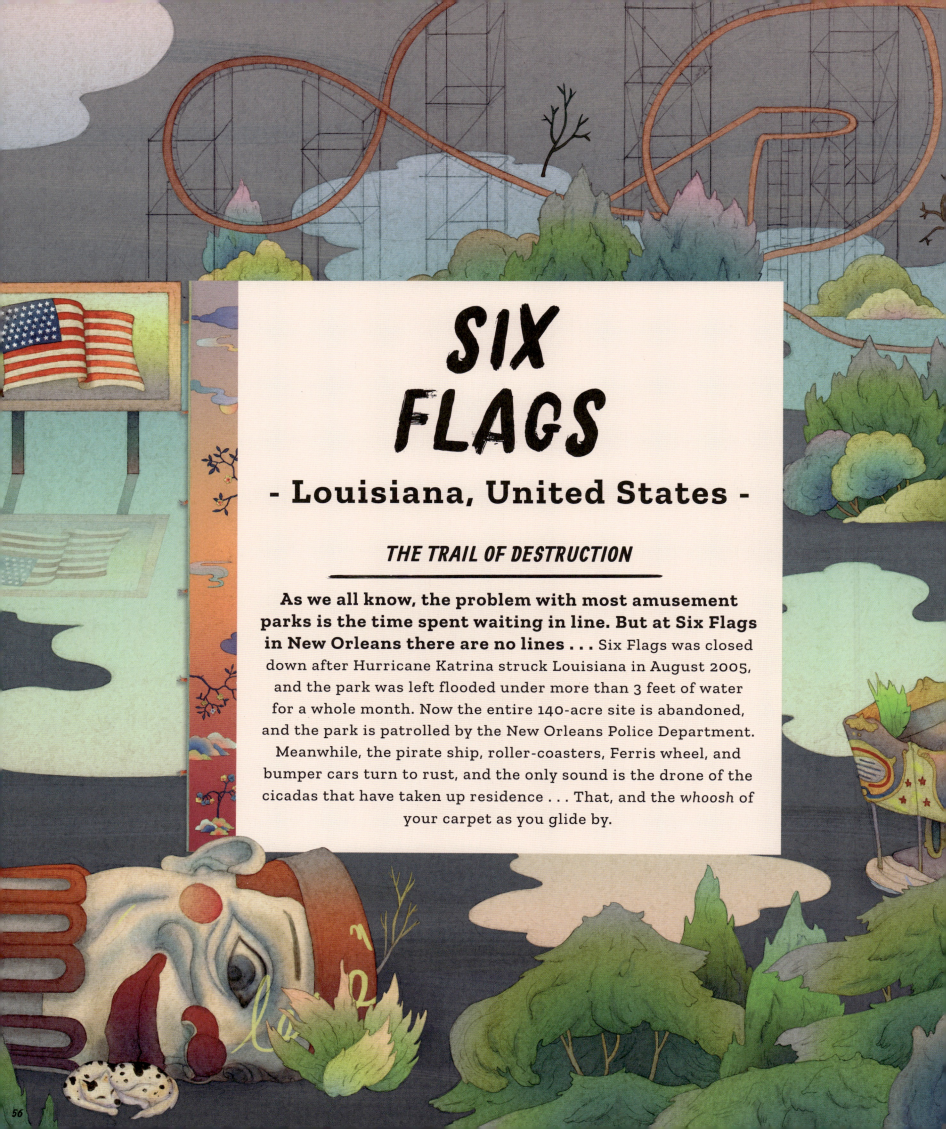

SIX FLAGS

- Louisiana, United States -

THE TRAIL OF DESTRUCTION

As we all know, the problem with most amusement parks is the time spent waiting in line. But at Six Flags in New Orleans there are no lines . . . Six Flags was closed down after Hurricane Katrina struck Louisiana in August 2005, and the park was left flooded under more than 3 feet of water for a whole month. Now the entire 140-acre site is abandoned, and the park is patrolled by the New Orleans Police Department. Meanwhile, the pirate ship, roller-coasters, Ferris wheel, and bumper cars turn to rust, and the only sound is the drone of the cicadas that have taken up residence . . . That, and the *whoosh* of your carpet as you glide by.

THE BIG SCREEN

If you thought an abandoned park would make a great setting for a movie, you'd be right. Parts of *Jurassic World* and *Percy Jackson: Sea of Monsters* were filmed here. Don't get any ideas, though: Entering the park is strictly prohibited unless you have special permission.

FUTURE PLANS

Since the park closed, many people have come up with ideas for what to do with the space—including turning it into a shopping center or reopening it as a new theme park—but nothing has happened yet.

NATURE TAKES OVER

Nature is gradually reclaiming the park, as plants—including trees—have begun to grow on some of the rides. Wild animals, such as boar, snakes, and even alligators, have also started to make the theme park their home.

JAZZLAND

The park first opened in 2000 under the name Jazzland, since New Orleans is widely regarded as the birthplace of jazz.

NATURAL DISASTER

Katrina was one of the worst hurricanes in U.S. history, causing up to 160 billion U.S. dollars—worth of damage to property and the death of at least 1,800 people.

VALLEY OF DEATH

- Kamchatka, Russia -

THE HAZARDOUS CANYON

As you might expect from the name, there's a very good reason why tourists aren't allowed into Kamchatka's Valley of Death . . . While guileless hikers might not spot much cause for concern at first in this remote volcanic gorge, they'll soon discover that the air here is filled with invisible poisonous gases that can kill without warning. As one animal strays into the area and dies, so another one follows, all attracted by the chance of eating the one before. Bears, foxes, wolverines, eagles, and lynxes have all met their deaths here. So be sure to steer your magic carpet at a safe altitude . . .

PREDATORS AND PREY

Due to the mix of gases here, animal carcasses take a long time to decay . . . and therefore a long time to stop attracting other animals. When the valley was discovered, over 200 carcasses of animals and birds were collected. Animals such as rodents and small birds were most common, but even animals as big as bears, foxes, and eagles were found in the Valley of Death.

BOILING HOT

The Valley of Death measures approximately 6,500 by 1,600 feet. It lies at the foot of the Kikhpinych Volcano and 4 miles from the Valley of Geysers, which is an area with more than 40 geysers (springs that jet hot water).

A CLOSE CALL

The deadly valley was only discovered in 1975 when vulcanologist V. L. Leonov stumbled across an area littered with animal corpses. A place nearby had previously been studied by geologists but the Valley of Death remained unknown. Even more worrying, the main part of the valley—known as the Main Death Ground (MDG)—was located less than 1,000 feet from a hikers' rest stop!

POISONOUS FUMES

The reason this valley is deadly to anyone who enters it is due to a high concentration of dangerous gases, such as hydrogen sulfide, carbon dioxide, and carbon disulfide.

A SAFE VIEWPOINT

Visitors without a magic carpet can only view the Valley of Death from the safety of a special observation deck, which has been built a safe distance away.

WARNING SIGNS

If scientists working in the area experience headaches, overheating temples, dizziness, or general weakness, then they know to get out fast! Often, they will climb up in altitude to get some fresh air and will recover relatively quickly from the dangerous fumes.

THE SVALBARD GLOBAL SEED VAULT

- Spitsbergen, Norway -

THE SEEDS OF SALVATION

Everyone knows that animals can go extinct like the dinosaurs did, but what about plants? And, perhaps more importantly, what about the plants we eat? To make sure this doesn't happen, the Svalbard Global Seed Vault has been created deep inside a mountain on a remote island, halfway between mainland Norway and the North Pole. The vault currently holds backup seeds from more than a million different crop varieties, from all over the world. To make sure the seeds are kept safe, private visits inside the vault are not allowed. And though you might feel tired after flying your carpet such a distance to get here, be sure to stay alert to the potential threat of polar bears as you approach!

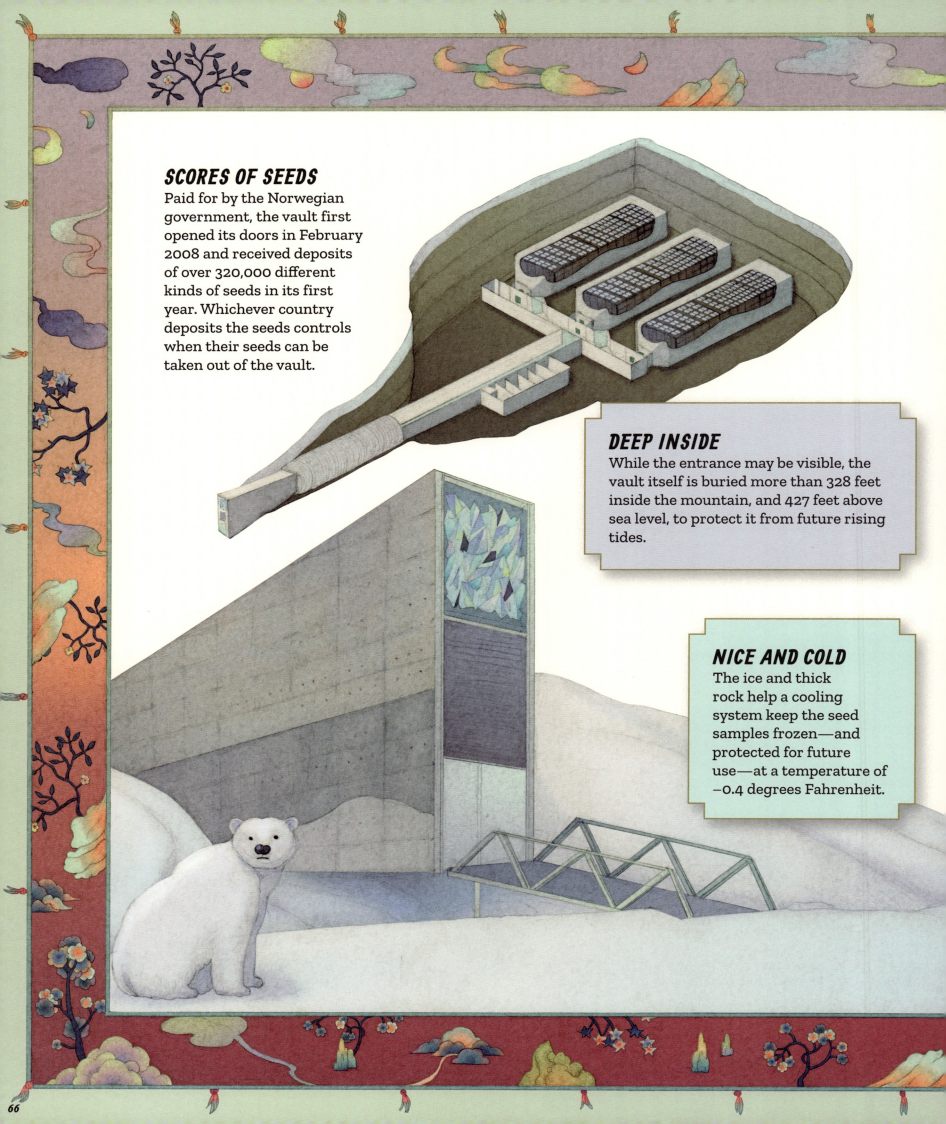

SCORES OF SEEDS

Paid for by the Norwegian government, the vault first opened its doors in February 2008 and received deposits of over 320,000 different kinds of seeds in its first year. Whichever country deposits the seeds controls when their seeds can be taken out of the vault.

DEEP INSIDE

While the entrance may be visible, the vault itself is buried more than 328 feet inside the mountain, and 427 feet above sea level, to protect it from future rising tides.

NICE AND COLD

The ice and thick rock help a cooling system keep the seed samples frozen—and protected for future use—at a temperature of −0.4 degrees Fahrenheit.

A BUNKER FOR PLANTS

There are more than 1,700 gene banks around the world, but Svalbard is the back up for all of them in case of war, accident, equipment malfunction . . . The vault has been built to withstand any kind of natural or human-made disaster.

PLENTY OF ROOM

The vault can store 4.5 million varieties of crops and a maximum of 2.5 billion individual seeds. The vault currently holds close to a million samples, with varieties from all over the world. This makes it the most diverse collection of food crop seeds in the world.

FAR AWAY

Svalbard is the furthest distance to the north a person can fly on a commercial flight, so it is about as far away from the rest of the world as it is possible to be.

THE AMBER ROOM

- Unknown Location -

THE "EIGHTH WONDER OF THE WORLD"

Given as a gift to Peter the Great of Russia in 1716 and installed in the sumptuous Catherine Palace in 1755, the Amber Room is made almost entirely out of a see-through gemstone called—you guessed it— amber. Valued at up to $500 million, the Amber Room would be an amazing sight to behold . . . if anyone knew where to find it! When the Nazis invaded the Soviet Union in 1941, they looted Catherine Palace and shipped the amber panels back to a castle in Germany—and that's where the story ends. Despite the many theories, nobody knows what happened to the panels after the end of the war . . . Perhaps all that's needed to track them down is a magic carpet and a bit of luck?

HIDDEN TREASURE

During the Second World War, Nazi soldiers were famously tasked with finding priceless art and transporting it back to Germany. The Nazis were known for hiding valuable items in very hard-to-reach places and did not document where they were being kept.

A FAILED PLOT

As the Nazi forces approached Catherine Palace, officials tried to hide the amber panels behind a layer of wallpaper—but the soldiers weren't fooled. They tore down the Amber Room and packed it up into 27 crates to be shipped to Königsberg Castle in Germany, where it reportedly went on display for two years.

NAZI PLUNDER

It's thought that the Nazis looted around one in five of all the artworks in Europe, including famous works by old masters such as Raphael, Vermeer, and Michelangelo, as well as modern masterpieces by Van Gogh, Klimt, and Pissarro. Experts estimate that around 100,000 pieces are yet to be recovered, including objects in crystal and silver.

AMBER RESIN

Amber is actually fossilized tree resin and sometimes has small animals and plants encased in it—just like in *Jurassic Park*. Over six tons of amber were used to construct the Amber Room's contents, such as its beautifully ornate paneling.

SUNKEN TREASURE

Many believe the panels were accidentally destroyed by the Soviet Army during a 1944 air raid on Königsberg Castle, while others reported watching the panels being loaded on board a Nazi ship called the *Wilhelm Gustloff*, which was sunk by a Soviet submarine in 1945.

THE SECOND AMBER ROOM

A reconstruction of the room—also in amber—began in Catherine Palace in 1979. It finally opened to visitors in 2003.

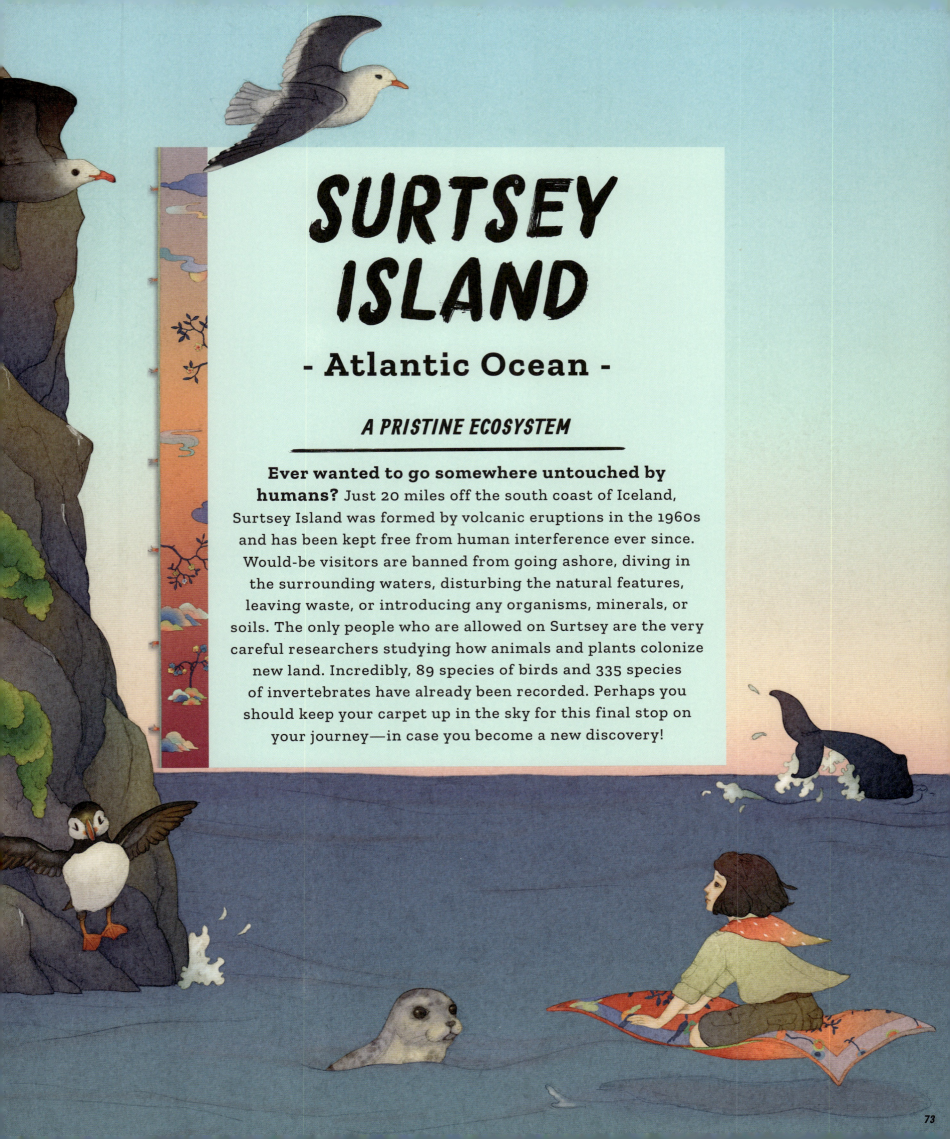

SURTSEY ISLAND

- Atlantic Ocean -

A PRISTINE ECOSYSTEM

Ever wanted to go somewhere untouched by humans? Just 20 miles off the south coast of Iceland, Surtsey Island was formed by volcanic eruptions in the 1960s and has been kept free from human interference ever since. Would-be visitors are banned from going ashore, diving in the surrounding waters, disturbing the natural features, leaving waste, or introducing any organisms, minerals, or soils. The only people who are allowed on Surtsey are the very careful researchers studying how animals and plants colonize new land. Incredibly, 89 species of birds and 335 species of invertebrates have already been recorded. Perhaps you should keep your carpet up in the sky for this final stop on your journey—in case you become a new discovery!

CLOSE CONTACT

The closest the average person can get to a good look at Surtsey (without getting in a huge amount of trouble!) is by looking out the window of a plane as it flies by the island.

A NATURE HAVEN

The island is home to a whole host of animals, including seals, puffins, gulls, fulmars, and guillemots, as well as slugs, spiders, and beetles. Birds began to nest on the island three years after the eruptions ended and began to use plants to make nests. A colony of gulls has been seen on the island since 1984, while Atlantic puffins have only been nesting there since 2004.

THE GOD OF FIRE

There's a good reason that Surtsey was named after Surtur, a Norse god of fire. It was formed from volcanic eruptions that produced a column of ash more than 5.5 miles high!

A WONDER OF SCIENCE

Surtsey is listed on the UNESCO World Heritage Site due to its great scientific value as a "pristine natural laboratory" that provides scientists with information about how plants and animals colonize new land.

GUANO FERTILIZER

The growth of the seabird population is very important as their poop—called guano—acts as an important fertilizer for any plants on the island. The first plant to grow on Surtsey sprouted in the spring of 1965. Moss started to appear in 1967, followed by the growth of lichens in 1970. Within the first 20 years of the island's existence, 20 species of plants were identified.

ERODING AWAY

The undersea volcanic eruption that formed the island lasted from November 1963 to June 1967. Coastal erosion has already halved the size of the island, and it is predicted that it will remove another two-thirds of land before it begins to slow.

Further information:

AMERICAN MUSEUM OF NATURAL HISTORY
Find out more about people, animals, and cultural artifacts around the world and through history.
amnh.org

ATLAS OBSCURA
An online guide to the world's hidden wonders.
atlasobscura.com

NATIONAL PARK SERVICE
Discover what natural wonders can be found in your area.
nps.gov

NATIONAL TRUST FOR HISTORIC PRESERVATION
Learn about historic preservation across the United States.
savingplaces.org

THE SMITHSONIAN INSTITUTION
Explore art, history, culture, and science through one of the world's largest museums.
si.edu

UNESCO WORLD HERITAGE LIST
Find out more about many of the locations in this book—and other protected places around the globe.
whc.unesco.org

The illustrations were created in pen and ink and colored digitally.
Set in Poster Brush, Ranga, and Zilla Sla.

Library of Congress Control Number 2020939749
ISBN 978-1-4197-5159-2

Text copyright © 2021 Patrick Makin
Illustrations copyright © 2021 Whooli Chen
Book design by Nicola Price
Edited by Jenny Broom
Cover © 2021 Magic Cat

Printed and bound in China
10 9 8 7 6 5 4 3 2 1

Abrams Books are available at special discounts when purchased in quantity for premiums and promotions as well as fundraising or educational use. Special editions can also be created to specification. For details, contact specialsales@abramsbooks.com or the address below.

ABRAMS The Art of Books
195 Broadway, New York, NY 10007
abramsbooks.com